LossSongs

Poems on Love Lost

Anora Sutherland

2015

Inner River Press
North Carolina, USA

LossSongs

Anora Sutherland

Copyright © 2015 Anora Sutherland

All rights reserved.

ISBN-10: 0982919131
ISBN-13: 978-0-9829191-3-2

Edition 3 April 2016

Cover photographs licensed from Canadian artist photographer Paula Dawn Lietz. www.pdlietzphotography.com

Cover design by Anora Sutherland

Inner River Press
A micro-press
The Piedmont, North Carolina
USA

www.innerriverpress.com
editor@innerriverpress.com

To those who navigate love's white waters,
as exciting and dangerous as the Potomac's Great Falls…

Contents

Prelude i
When the Rain Comes Down 1
Grip of Fear 3
Staying 4
Dangling Heart 5
Crow Stones 7
Refrains 9
Emblem of Apollo 10
Apollo 11
   (I) 11
   (II) 12
   (III) 13
   (IV) 14
   (V) 15
   (VI) 16
   (VII) 17
   (VIII) 18
   (IX) 19
   (X) 20
   (XI) 21
Athena 22
Illumining 23
Instrument 25
Resolute 26
More 27
Seeing 28
Tripped 30
Notes 31
   When the Rain Comes Down 31
   Grip of Fear 32
   Staying 32
   Dangling Heart 33
   Crow Stones 33
   Refrains 34
   Emblem of Apollo 34
   Apollo (I – XI) 34
   Athena 35
   Illumining 36
   Instrument 36

    Resolute 37
    More 38
    Seeing 38
    Tripped 40
Afterthoughts 41
Acknowledgements 45
Anora Sutherland 47
Paula Dawn Lietz 49

Prelude

Hearts yearn for the spell of love.
Mine was no exception.

Falling in love as a teenager, one lays roots and grows vines that may twist about beautifully and distressingly through years to come. Some marry young, and if lucky make it through the decades. When our marriages crack and break, those we left behind are those we come back to find.

&

When I was a fourteen I fell in love so deeply that it permeated my dreams, sleeping and waking. A love so resonant, it was like living in an additional dimension – harmonically rich, complex, beguiling. This was the kind of happening that psychics, psychologists and psychiatrists study. It would take half a lifetime for me to sort through.

I have hesitated to share my story, not wanting for people to idealize it as something to want. I always had read longingly about the intense love between creative people - artists, writers and musicians. It's not for the faint of spirit, if it is even a choice.

&

Soon after my love was reciprocated, my father received orders to move from Washington DC to North Africa. It was 1974. I was sixteen.

I cried myself over the Atlantic, and all through our family visit in Rome.

I wouldn't know it then, or for years, but I was not only grieving leaving behind my sweetheart, the loss had tapped years of loss. My family never stayed in one place for very long: the daughter of an American diplomat, we moved, and moved, and moved. We made friends, left friends and were left by friends over and over and over, year after year, secretly establishing a deep underground reservoir of pure grief.

&

In those days, friendships were cut short or put on hold by distances. Phone calls were prohibitively expensive. Letters took a week or more. No Internet. No texting. Telegrams, the equivalent of texts in a way, were charged by the character, and very expensive. They were resorted to in times of need for money, illness, marriage, births and deaths. Whatever contact friends had before, with distance we knew silence and our imaginations.

&

Returning from North Africa and Italy where I finished high school, we would have a special month house sitting in my dance teacher's Beacon St. apartment catching a lot of live music in Boston. He would ask me to move south so we could be together, but my parents had already paid for me to enter college, and it was a week away.

Wrestling with an open relationship, a friendship, being lovers, not being lovers, was like stepping and slipping on rocks in a stream. How to navigate the distance? What to do with the feelings?

We would cross paths again and again, but never live in the same town again. Despite, or perhaps because of all the moves, this fascination, this complex connection remained through the years. At times in touch, at others no word for long periods. At times aspiring to be sweethearts again, at others, trying to be friends.

Who can say what might have happened if we had ever lived in the same place. We could have easily rung ourselves dry, crashed on the rocks, as happens to so many. Without the chance to know, with the random rewards and pains of long distance, imagination played.

&

I would study Chinese at University and travel to Taiwan and China, marry a gregarious Chinese student in Massachusetts, and have a son.

Learn to speak and cook and play Chinese. The marriage would find relief in divorce just after the 10th anniversary.

Nothing could have prepared me for the grief that would come.

&

It was exactly twenty years since I had left the Washington DC area in 1974 that my son and I would move from "up north." My mother had a home we could share.

My father, who was also temporarily "stateside" in the area with his second wife, was given six months from diagnosis of cancer.

The polar caps melted. The underground grief reservoirs flooded to the surface. I cried every day like afternoon tropical storms.

Six months later, I spent his last day at his bedside in the hospital on Gallows Road. The call would come in at 4:20 am. At 5:00 I would tell a dear friend who was staying, the first person I would tell, and after she hugged me, I remembered that I had been there for the birth of her son earlier in the year. A karmic circle.

&

In reconnecting with long ago friends from high school in the area, old sweetheart paths would cross again. Friends. Possibilities. Something promising, then disappointing. Then a spark. Then none. On it went.

&

I would find my way into twelve step programs, still grieving from all the losses, but also healing.

My son and I settled into Sundays with a local spiritual community. Just the right fit: Tibetan Buddhist.

A stranger's phone call announced the suicide of my father's second wife, and, an estate sale of my father's belongings. A storm of emotions tied me in knots – grief and anger, and despair.

Contrary to suggestion, not a year after getting sober, I was taking vows and robes of a (non-resident) Buddhist nun (in America). I could still raise my son, and try making a living. It was very unusual, definitely uncommon, possibly crazy, yet somehow so organic a step for me. For my son, it was much less clear, though it would lead to unforgettable adventures across country.

The chapbook begins here.

It is 1998. My son and I are in the Southwest, living in a mobile home. I'm a nun with prayer practices and weekly services living independently, raising my son, taking him to school, skate board play dates with friends, mountain biking, hiking, cooking dinners…

The poems that follow are like the shards that archeologists study; though incomplete they tell a story.

Anora Sutherland

Olive Chapel Road, Apex
North Carolina's Piedmont
United States of America

Whence comes this torrent spring
that would fill the Roman aqueducts?

AS

When the Rain Comes Down

Where does my mind go
Where does my heart go
Where does my breath go
When the rain comes down

Why do I disappear
Why do I feel such fear
Why do I come unclear
When the rain comes down

Waking in the night
You're in my dreams again
You come like a spell
And take hold

I try to let go
To move on, to forget
Your unwavering grip
On my soul

When the rain comes down
The rain comes down
The rain comes down

Heavy air and humidity weighs
Spits of rain hitting my face
There's no way this is possible
Why can't I erase

I wake up in the night
Dreaming of you
I wake in a sweat
I know we're not yet through

But you're in love with her
And I have taken vows
Shaved my head and moved out West
There's no way this makes sense

The rain still falls
The rain falls still
The rainfall stills

There is something unfinished between us
Between now and when we die
Something to help heal us
Though I do not know what

I need to spend some time with you
There's something I've got to face
I'm sorry to have to ask
But I cannot erase

My mind is here
My heart is here
My breath is here
The rain has run its ground

When
Will you come to town?

Sunday, September 27, 1998 10:06 PM

Grip of Fear

(a request of him)

Gentle with your distance girl
Her heart though big does tremble
No promise for tomorrow's needed but
The grip of fear's not simple.

Though never would she bind you
Or tell you what to do
When you speak of lady friends
Her gut turns curly queues.

She trusts you with her safety
Sailed with you far from shore
Still she shivers, fog horn bellows
The warning signals toll.

So if you can, and if you will
Her heart is all a tremble
Do not speak of lady friends
The grip of fear's not simple.

So if you can and if you will
Guide her through the shoals
Speak some words of reassurance
The grip of fear's not simple.

Spring 2003

Staying

You called my name today
A slow and measured phrase
Each sound filled with heart.

I replayed your voice
Again and again,
Not a hint this was the end.

You told me
How sad I looked
My poker face exposed
My bravery failed.

Tears slid over my lashes
Cheeks held still as I could
Breath frozen to hide
My grief…

A sadness so deep
So repeated
Too many years now.

I was always sad when you left
But I was even sad before you came
Because you always went.

Sad that I wanted you.
Sad that you didn't stay.
Sad that the love stayed warm.
Sad.

I heard you call my full name today
With love, with heart, with hope.
I cried remembering how much I'd tried
To keep you.

You just won't stay.
I live and breathe with this dull ache.

November 2005

Dangling Heart

You hang my heart each time
You choose to come.
You allot your days,
How long you'll stay,
When you'll go.
My only choice is to say no.

I'll say yes, and you'll come
And when you go…

You'll leave my heart hanging
And I'll have to heal it again
To seal it and en-whole it
Until I don't give a shit
Don't care what you do.

(But I don't tell you.)

So you'll knock again,
As if we can still be friends,
By phone or by mail
And I'll say welcome
Believing in my fairy tale

I imagine you'll stay
And love more, and complete

Our story.

You
Feed on my attention
My devotion
My patient
Compliance.

And each time you go,
My aching heart tolls.
The church bells peal
The end.

LossSongs – Anora Sutherland

I think its grief.
But that's only true
Because I disengage
The rage that tears through.
(That would close you out
Forever.)

So what's my part?
I always put it on you.

Now I see I leave behind
A dangling heart
Slung from the line

Dangling as it were free.

I want to throw the blame on you.
But my conscience is too aware
I must bear my share.

I fed my attention to you
My devotion,
My patient compliance.

There could be no hanging
No hanging heart
If there was no…
No dangling start.

October 2005

Crow Stones

Every gem I find
I want for you

Wishing you happy
Radiant, strong
Your agony, healed, gone.

~

Searching for shiny stones
Gems of knowing for your suffering
I set them at your window sill

Eyes alert for reflected light
Delivering mica, quartz and geode
An offering of Crow stones

Trained in Crow's ways
To give the best away
Over and over again

~

Every gem I find
I want for you

Wanting you happy
Radiant, strong
Your angst, healed, gone.

~

But wanting you happy
Doesn't mean you are,
You can, or will be.
Or I am.

No.
Not happy.
Not I.
Nor you.

What is it
We so seek?

Is it more than just an ease?
An OK with now?
An acceptance
A lightness
A breath that
Cannot quit
Feeding
Fueling
Caring
Soothing?

A breath that stays
That prays
And knows
There is an answer?

~

Each and every gem I find
I want for you.

Hoping you're happy,
Radiant, strong.
Your heartache, healed, gone.

~

Eyes alert for reflected light
Scouting mica, quartz and geode
Crow stones for your window sill.

Trained in Crow's ways
To give the best away
Over and over again

Refrains

How am I to know who you are to me?

Are you my heart?
My mate?
My soul?
My fate?

A human habit?
My white rabbit?
A synoptic pathway
In gray matter?

Or are you everything?
Or nothing?

Or no one…

Just someone pretty
Who sang his pain
And caught my heart
In his refrain?

Such a longing for you
Who are not mine to hold.
Such a misplaced caring
Misguided, untoward.

Emblem of Apollo

You, who you really are
And who I held you to be
My boy, the rebel, the man
The emblem of Apollo
You wear the prize of my mother's son;
Your blue eyes
Stun me

Whoever you are
Whatever you do
This flickering love
Comes through

There is no protection
From the fear that haunts you
From the love that taunts you
That you'll disappear
If you keep a lover near

You are a man now
You cannot be engulfed
You are King, Zeus, Jupiter
You will not be ruled

There I go again
Speaking to the sky
A ghost from long ago
Still tricking my mind

Who you really were I'll never know
But I can claim what I held you to be
And know my hazel eyes glow bright
And I'm every bit as much as I need to be

Apollo

(I)

Whether far or near
What a spell you were!

Eternally young
Your eyes such a blue
Your body waxed and sinewed.

Your hair like spun light
Dazzling.

Your strength, breathtaking
Your intelligence,
Startling.

Oh how you shone.

(II)

The mortal maidens want you.

You tease and you play.
So gorgeous
We cannot resist.

You were born to love
And love you do.

You sparkle,
Eyes burning like the sun,
Mesmerizing.

(III)

Born of the Gods,

We imagine you always get yours

Then leave.

Is that true?

(IV)

You,
Who you really are,
And
Who I held you to be

My boy,
The rebel,
The goddened man,

You bear the prize of my mother's son

Your blue eyes
Stun me.

(V)

After decades,
Of loving
And refusing

You've changed the rules
Immortal you!

To stay near
I will have to
Dampen my passion into
Sisterly affection for you

A relation you'll allow
In the dark, in whispers.

Comfortable for you
It seems
You continue in my dreams

Stoke in me a fire
I tend constantly
To be safe

As if dozing by burning embers
Or serpents
In the temple.

(VI)

You split
Your love in two:
Passion for your lovers
Trust for another.

By Zeus and Leto
I swear
You need no protection.

The fear that haunts you
That you'll be lost
If trusting a lover
With your flaws
Has no ground.

Immortal! You
Cannot be taken down,
Engulfed, swallowed.

You are King, son of Zeus,
Rest assured.
You will not be ruled
You prevail.

Stop, I say to you, dear one
Stop dividing your love in two.

(VII)

Apollo?

Are you there?

Was that you?

(VIII)

I'm speaking to the sky again.

A ghost from long ago,
Yet flickering inside.

(IX)

Apollo

You are immortal to me

The light from your gaze

Alchemistry.

(X)

Where you travel
I cannot know.

You visit no more
In my night.

Be well.

(XI)

Athena came.

The spell is broken;
My hazel eyes glowing flames.

She gave me wings.

The sky is heaven.

Athena

At Santa Maria sopra Minerva in Assisi Italy

Athena, Minerva, Glaukopis
Goddess of a hundred names
Patroness of a thousand towns
Bearer of ancient powers
How have we survived so long ignoring you?

Too few know you
So far were you were exiled.
Your strength challenging mortal men
The Christians esteemed meek Mary instead.

Were it not for my visit to Assisi
Where your ancient temple stood intact
I would not have remembered to ask you
To release me from the quicksand lands.

Roman columns and pediment
Ancient stones and ancient strength
The Christians merely removed your likeness
Added paintings and changed the name

"Santa Maria sopra Minerva"

Athena
You are not who they said you were
They lied.
The Christians cast you out
To keep women down.

Now I know
Like Joe Hill, you are
Never dying, always alive.

Illumining

Your songs spring from my heart
Like the ring of chimes
At wind's start

In moments surprising:
Waking me
Shaking me
Making me
Wish I did not know you.

Every word you've chosen
In your lyrics, your poetry
Links you to me.

The sun was setting
Beyond the talling pines
Its light upon the tattered bark…

Illumined.

~

Illumined…

It's a golden word

A golden sword

A golden key
That unlocks
The darkened space
Where your songs were shut away.

Your lyrics spill across
The mirror of my mind
Cutting the glass with an edge so fine
I feel that I will break.

Out it comes, your clear refrain
"Illumined with a different sort of love"

Lighting upon me like a branchless dove
Clasping me
With piercing beauty.

Your words, your lyrics,
Bind me.

~

As the sun illumines
With a quieting glow,
A darkening shine,
I sit crafting these lines
Countering the spell of the chimes.

December 2005

Instrument

I am your unwitting resonant
The one in whom your sound unfolds.

Resolute

I hear your voice
the warmth you've grown
the heart you now dare show
your music, delicate and rich
inviting our senses to open.

I see your pictures
scan your face
remembering when
we were teenagers,
going back forty years.

Though I miss you -
hate to let you go;
though I carry an ache
in my heart, 'n my skin
and my bone,

we were lovers,
not friends,
you don't get to choose how this ends.

Now that I have the strength to
bear the loss,
accepting less
is not even possible.

If I never
see you in person again,
feel your eyes within my own
brace my wary breast
against the ground of your chest,

I am resolute
nothing less will do.

More

I couldn't take
What you couldn't give
Baby I gotta have more

It's not that I'm greedy
Or that I'm needy
It's just I'm a woman
Not a whore.

Seeing

We meet between
Then and when
There and where

Both of us, thickened and grayed
Wrinkled and worn

You invite a hug
I adhere to form
But nothing like my surrender
At ten plus four

When your two years older
Was like a dozen
And you were everything
I wanted to be but wasn't

We meet because
We've always met again
Trying to be friends
Though one or the other
Is never content

Sitting for tea
I turn my eyes to see
Blue eyes, gray speckled goatee
You look like my brother staring back at me

I blink
I'm afraid
Like twins now
You look the same

Turn away
Turn back
Blink my eyes again

~

LossSongs – Anora Sutherland

My mother is walking
My baby brother and me
When I was one or two or three

The walkers-by stopped to say.
My what beautiful blue eyes
And blond hair he has

Their gaze missing mine
Brown haired, brown eyed and plain
He can't be yours, they'd exclaim

Mom, brown haired and eyed,
Smiles and sighs.
My husband's family
Has the fairer coloring

They think I don't understand
If they think of me at all
I was only one or two or three

But I'll fall in love with blonds
With blue eyes for decades
Before awakening

~

Soon it's time to go
You don't know what I saw
And I don't say.

Tripped

Comes a time
That a single phrase
Can throw the switch
Blow the circuit

Don't need a knife
Or a gun, or a girl
Or a bet or a debt
Or a punch or a habit

Comes a time
When we get clear
We know what's what

Comes that time
When a tone of voice
Just unforgiving enough

Trips the breaker
Throws the switch
Blows the circuit.

Notes

When the Rain Comes Down

There are mysteries in life and death, in the deep dark heavens, in the earth's boiling depths. Mysteries in love and hate, loss and redemption. Mysteries in the complexities of human hearts and minds and souls; our biologies; in connections and disconnections.

The bond between two lovers is so multi-layered. Visual. Energetic. Tactile. Historical. Biological. Soulful.

What makes for its depth? What causes an ending to not feel final? What is unfinished business in a former relationship?

Dreams, like confessions, can surface threads that need to be woven into the weave, placed in their place, not left to unravel.

This song-like poem emerged suddenly one evening, ready formed, as many of my pieces, swiftly, merely, I think now, because I withhold my writing until it just bursts out.

A country song had come on the speakers while standing in Walmart in Cottonwood, Arizona. A man was singing about a love he hadn't done right. Right then and there, as music has the power to do, a spell fell over me, reawakening what was. On an evening soon after, When the Rain Comes Down fell out onto the paper, interrupting my transcription work. That awareness captured in the poem led to action.

Time would permit reconnections, but would also reveal incompatibilities that a young heart wouldn't understand: differing desires, lifestyles, personalities and realities.

Reconnecting created moments of meaning and closeness, and difficult ones. Sometimes they were like the dark swollen waters of the Potomac racing on a winter night, ready, with one slip of a foot, to take you into eternity. Other times they were filled with silent reverence with the gentle cracks of twigs and dry leaves in the fall woods, when a giant owl spreads its wings and soars across the path.

Harmony in love did not come with the asking. Oh how I wish it did.

Grip of Fear

This poem, like a number of my poems, popped, almost like hatching out of an egg, or splitting from a pea pod.

I was seeking some gentle way to ask for help in overcoming jealousy - the fear of losing one's love to another. In sharing the fear, the focus was not to criticize, but instead to ask for help in overcoming the fright that had arisen.

It would be hard not to hear that as criticism. So I silenced this and it lay in waiting for the realm of poetry, the safe space in which to speak.

Fear is not easy to dispel. Once it takes hold it can take over - and thus the words:

> "the grip of fear's not simple."

"Distance girl" refers to being a long distance girlfriend.

Staying

Some relationships are confusing. There's love, but no staying power. Always the impulse to go. Yet, also, the impulse to return. This poem is about the deep sadness and ambivalence that permeated the relationship.

The poem also speaks to the core wound of people in a highly mobile life. Just like plants whose roots are torn when pulled from the ground, so too our roots are torn when pulled from a place where we have developed relationships, where we have established a life.

Normal McCaig who coined the term "Global Nomad" was the first person whose writings I read that spoke about the tremendous unprocessed grief that people who grew up like me carry, mostly unconsciously.

So much more was at play here than just one high school sweetheart relationship that was renewed post-divorce. This relationship was fueled with many of my core unconscious wounds as I would learn in the years to come, mostly through writing poetry.

Dangling Heart

This dependence in love, this need, is not determined by what gender we are, but instead by something very fundamental like how we feel in our skin, whether we have felt loved or not, at the very core of ourselves, in our cells, in our nervous system, in the very ocean of our being.

I have seen the compromise of continuing a once romantic relationship, or a potentially romantic relationship. We've reassured the other, the one desired as lover, or the one who wants to be our lover, that we can be friends. We just don't want it to end. But beneath it all, one still wants more. Our spirits rise and fall with semi-conscious disappointment and guilt.

Owning one's part in a situation which isn't as one wants it is key to making personal change. Understanding my part was a breakthrough.

Crow Stones

Every time I learned something deep, something meaningful, something healing, I would have an instantaneous response to share it, knowing it would be helpful to him, as it was helpful to me.

It was a reflex - focusing on someone else's pain, helping distract me from my own.

Breaking the habit of always turning to another to share my insight even if my intentions were good, proved so difficult.

Refrains

Captivated at such a haunting level, I had to examine what was going on; tackle the mystique of falling in love, all the romance and dance around it, trying to understand why I was so attached.

On the one hand, sorting through the possibilities felt clarifying, and yet on the other, it didn't neutralize the gravitational force. I was powerless for so long.

Emblem of Apollo

"Emblem of Apollo" was the poem from which the Apollo series emerged. I explored the insight I might gain from immortalizing the lover in mythic terms. I explored the power of blue eyes, the difference between who I beheld a person to be, and who they actually were; their different roles in my life and my psyche.

I could acknowledge the on-again off-again love – or at least that the signal was "flickering" through. I came to understand the behavior of keeping a confidant separate from a lover to protect oneself, to avoid being engulfed by a woman. Since mothers most often raise their sons, breaking free into one's own as a young man must be hard and complicated. This poem also raises themes which the following poems continue.

Apollo (I – XI)

These poems are notes to Apollo, as a metaphor for the young man I had adored. Seeing a love in light of a god or goddess was a way of gaining perspective on it. Exaggerate something to make it clearer, then take it back down to size.

Apollo is a "Pretty Man" as poet and playwright Marcy Corprew speaks of in "Man Pretty," and women respond to "Pretty Men" in many ways that do not support who they are, just as I'm sure, men are caught in the spells of "Pretty Women."

Athena

My mother's mother passed away in Italy where she had lived out her years as widow of an Italian diplomat, my grandfather. When she died, my mother took her grandchildren, and their parents to Italy, for a once in a life time trip.

There, in Assisi, where St. Francis, the much-loved patron saint of animals, once lived, was a Roman temple that had been converted to a Catholic Church. They simply added St. Mary's name to the temple name, and changed the images inside. But outside it looks exactly like a Roman Temple, and inside, it does too.

Sometimes we need things to be really obvious to get the picture.

Growing up in the Middle East around the ruins of the Roman and Greek worlds, my parents had given me an ancient coin, (or a reproduction of one, one can never really tell), with Athena on one side; Athena, much like Lady Liberty on older American coins.

I had worked on a poem about Athena a few years ago for a joint show with writers and quilters called Narrative Threads, but it was too complex to be completed in time. I continued to weave away with the theme and subject of Athena. She was elusive. I shared the poem's start with Irish poet Christine Elizabeth Murray, and she suggested I get to know Athena from the inside out, not just the surface.

I was intrigued by how Athena was represented with an owl on her shoulder, and sometimes appeared to people as a bird, similar to the stories Christians tell about visits by birds who they saw as the Holy Spirit. Slowly I began awakening to the impact of the Christian banishing of the power of Roman gods, especially Athena, goddess of wisdom and war, for who they offered in exchange for us to adore, the forgiving, kind and mild St. Mary. It was a profound awakening, its light still showing me things I had not considered.

In writing the Apollo series. I began to recognize Athena as a counter force to Apollo, as the strong clear wise feminine spirit.

Illumining

Ah. This one.

After a relationship is over. We think all's well and we're done. Sometimes it is. And when it isn't, a little moment can be ground shaking.

Some poems mark a moment in time we wish never to forget. Others mark a moment in time we won't be able to forget.

It was a chilly late afternoon. Gazing over a finger of North Carolina's Lake Jordan as the sun was setting through the trees, I turned around and noticed the warm rays lighting the rough trunks of the pine trees around me.

In a flash, my writing-trained mind always seeking words for what my eyes see, the word "illumined" arose, where "lit" would have spared me the fanfare, and also this poem.

A beautiful and sharply cutting sensation arose as the difficult feelings of loss took hold. The word was tied to the lyrics of an old love's song and the whole song burst out of deep freeze and took over.

As writers, musicians and artists are in the habit of doing, taking what we experience and transforming it, metamorphosize it into something that both liberates us and makes an offering to others, I worked to shape this experience into something clearer than the muddy waters of inner sensations. It was too striking, too painful, and also too beautiful an experience to let float downstream unrecorded.

I had to find an intriguing way of naming it, describing it poetically in a way that might set me free. While I hurt, I also was excited to have this vivid experience showing me how my mind works. And even though writing about it makes it last longer, perhaps it also ensures that in the reading and telling of it, its grip will diminish over time.

Instrument

Something amazing happens when talking with a good listener. When they hear us; both what we say and what we don't say; when they take us all in.

Something profound was occurring: the power of witnessing, a spiritual exchange that leaves those involved feeling changed afterwards.

I had a moment's understanding about how a person's story or conversation reverberates inside the listener, and then is projected back with a specific amplification customized by the listener; the way a hollow guitar shape amplifies the sound of the strings.

As an introvert with some extrovert skills, I have done more than my share of listening. As the outsider I was over and over again, as our family changed countries and schools, traveling between the US and Italy and the Middle East, since I wasn't quick-spoken and funny like my siblings, instead of entertaining strangers to win friends, I listened empathetically.

In that listening, in responding to the emotional, felt experience of others, it's like being an acoustic guitar body, helping their sound resonate, and in so doing, allowing them to hear themselves differently, and often deeply.

Resolute

This poem draws a line. It marks a change of perspective. There came a time when being friends was not a choice, not even an option; a clarity emerged, a self-understanding.

Counselors and relationship professionals have told me for years that sustaining friendship after love affairs may always be painful and might be ill-advised. But cutting the connection felt like a death, and only became possible when it did, not when I wanted it to.

More

"More" is about really understanding that as a woman in love, it was only normal, right and healthy to want a full relationship. If lovers, then lovers be. If friends, then friends be, but not something funny in-between.

Using such a strong word as "whore" took some courage. Here I'm using it to refer to someone who is paid for personal services, and who could be paid to be a friend, or a sexual partner, or whatever in between, whatever the customer wants at the time.

I took some relief in this line, playing on the slang "I couldn't take" meaning "it was unbearable", and the literal meaning of not being able to receive what was not given:

> "I couldn't take what you couldn't give"

This is the beginning of a song. I became aware that songs had the power to alter and shift my spirit. As I wrestled to release the hold, or spell, or attachment, I reconnected with the Blues, and came to remember how singing the Blues releases "the blues."

Expressing the pain through vocalized sustained exhaling, singing, actually shifted the grief. Whether grief is expressed as a freezing of feelings of despair, or released through varying degrees of tears and sounds, the rhythm and the chord changes of Blues songs can swing and rock the singer out of the sense of despair.

Seeing

It took decades to gather and see the pieces of the puzzle that exposed my low self-worth in relation to my "beautiful" brother who was born 13 months after I was, with completely different, fair coloring, blond hair and blue eyes.

Our parents had brown hair and eyes. My mother tells us the doctor said, "Lady I don't know what you do in your afternoons," implying that the milkman or postman may have been involved. (Can you imagine?)

In 1978, when I was twenty, one piece emerged, when I answered a question about why I didn't get along with my brother. Out of nowhere conscious came, "My brother was beautiful." With that speaking an electric shock shivered all the way own my spine, as if tapping a painful memory when I was a toddler. That was one piece, his beauty, and in contrast my plainness.

But until the moment described in this poem, I only had an inkling about my attraction to blond haired blue eyed people and its connection to all the praise my brother received when I was a toddler.

It took seeing this old beau look so much like my brother that it scared me for me to awaken to the power of my toddler experience. The powerful unconscious force that had driven my attraction to blond haired blue eyed boys became tangible. As survival reflex - if blond & blue gets attention, then I must get me some blond & blue.

This awakening was similar to seeing the temple in Assisi, where the Roman Catholic Church simply changed the name of a Roman temple once dedicated to Minerva (Athena).

I could finally see how they cast out the strong goddess (with the pantheon of gods), and commanded devotion to Christian holy ones, Mary, Jesus' mother, in addition to the Holy Trinity of the Father, the Son and the Holy Ghost.

Though for years my family had walked and driven by hundreds of holy sites all around the Mediterranean, Roman, Greek, Christian, Moslem, and more, all the while repeatedly seeing how one culture replaces another, builds atop the ruins of a previous era, it took this one powerfully clear sight to bring home what had happened.

These are Rosetta stone moments, when a mystery is solved because something you know can be matched to something you don't know, and a whole previously secret world opens up.

Tripped

Relationships are a lot about circuits – how much tolerance each person has, when, for what, and at what point the charge exceeds what one circuit can bear.

This poem talks about a moment that tips the balance.

No two people have the exact same limits, and our limits and tolerance vary over time. I never know where my limits are until they happen.

It's like digging through the dirt, thinking you can keep digging because you've been digging, and then you hit granite. That's that. The ground is too hard to dig.

But it may not be granite though, it could just be the digger is exhausted in the hot noon day North Carolina sun.

Afterthoughts

Some say it is great fortune to know such an all-consuming love. I am not so sure.

When it's good, it is ecstasy.

When there is trouble, possible devastation.

&

Daddy shared with me one of the conversations he'd had with his father after grandmother suddenly died New Year's Eve 1957, just weeks before my birth.

"Was it worth it, after all, if love's loss leaves you in such pain? Would you do it all over again? Would you wish to love again?"

"Yes," grandfather answered. "Yes."

&

Falling in love reminds me of a very dangerous water sport. It's thrilling until it's devastating or over, leaving life dull and unsatisfying.

The forces of sexual love are as powerful as volcanos, earthquakes, tidal waves and hurricanes, and they happen inside us in our inner world, our inner universe.

Once a force is released, there is no bringing it home until it runs its course. The gravitational force between people for sex ensures the future of humanity. We are wired for attraction. Wired to be drawn into embrace. It is so deeply central to our beings that resisting the "fall" into love can feel impossible.

When the early stages are so exhilarating, with feeling high, euphoric and intoxicated, who would even wish to resist? Would that it were more than simply the instinct for continuity of our species. Would that it were sustainable, even a guarantee of a right match.

The battle between the rational, logical mind, and the evolutionarily informed heart continues. While some cultivate containing and guarding the heart. Others cultivate opening and following the heart. Neither path assures a happy life-long love relationship.

But for many of us, time proves that romantic love, sexual love with charm and grace, drama and danger, dissolves in the forces of common life. At least one out of two couples do not make it.

Admitting that falling in love holds no guarantee of a long term compatible relationship feels sacrilegious. If the mystical (or biological) experience of falling in love isn't the answer, what's the alternative? Is it a rational, planned relationship, similar to what families plan in traditional countries? Those who believe in "love," the kind that arises from "chemistry" or "attraction" and hopefully "compatibility" would rather die.

&

What is this kind of love? It can feel crazy, desperate. Fated. Some may question it as a fantasy, fiction or idle romance. Was it ordinary, or extraordinary? Was it healthy or did it cross over some line?

I have my theories about falling in love in that all-consuming way. I believe it may be due to incomplete development of self in the infant period of our lives. Insufficient mirroring. Insufficient reflection. Insufficient eyelight – the accepting and approving gaze from one being to another.

The idea is that we didn't fully separate from our parents, didn't complete the individuation process, and so seek to relocate that all-powerful love again in another person, hoping at last to find completion. For an infant, completion requires maintaining that merged connection until safely able to individuate. For a teenager, and young adult, completion requires the connection to be within oneself. If you didn't get that sense of completeness in infancy and the early years, that woundedness goes underground, survives the low contact years when affection from parents is reduced in the later grade school and early middle school years, and by the time puberty hits, teens might be so starved for attention and physical touch, it can be a powder keg ready to explode.

We find ourselves attracted to an individual, who, when it's intense enough an attraction, Harville Hendrix theorizes, reflects some aspect of our mother or father that awakens in us the possibility of getting the love we longed for. But it's so tall an order, and the object of our attraction comes loaded, as we do, with all kinds of triggers, that a sustainable affair is unlikely.

With that childhood woundedness, the unconscious focus goes into merging with the other person, similar to an infant's experience, where one's survival is dependent on understanding and relating to the parent figure intimately. We don't understand that merging is a transition, a rite of passage we have to walk through on the way to becoming whole as young adults, and it's not the end game.

In the swoon of bliss from renewing that depth of love and adoration, we are lost and want to continue that state forever. But we are stuck, trying to hold onto a moment, when we need to grow, come into our own and know a freedom and power as great as that adoration, but sourced in our connection with our deep inner spiritual selves.

Anora

August 2015

Acknowledgements

My mother Carol who loves me and creates beauty wherever she is. My father Peter who loved song and poetry, played guitar and performed. Thank you for the amazing life you gave us, full of creativity, learning languages and traipsing across the ancient empires of the world singing Peter Paul & Mary and Pete Seeger songs and listening to Mom read from *Le Guide Bleu*.

Camilla for being a wonderful aunt, always so cool, creative and pathfinding. My husband Martin, fellow global nomad, navigator of the future, and technology facilitator, for more than I could name. My son Jason who continues to astonish me with his creativity, depth, intelligence and inspiration. My creative and always interesting family:
Susan. Paul. Andrew. Hua. Maria. Natalia. Elizabeth.

My African American English teacher in high school,
Mrs. Snowden, for her encouraging note on my 10th grade creative writing project: "Write, write, and write. Don't ever stop writing!"

Martin Brossman for being a collaborator, mentor, coach and an all-around exceptional person; and guiding me through the transition from corporate employee to micro-business owner. We co-authored a business book, my first.

My dear friend Kevy who died before she was meant to.
My close friends whose lives are not obsessed with being artists:
Sue M., Lenora, Laura, Joan, Sharon, Elaine.

My fellow artists, writers, poets, songwriters and performers, without you, who knows if this could come to be. Thank you for your example, your inspiration, your explanations and encouragement. Below, naming but a few of the many of have come my way:

Nancy. C. Elizabeth. Leslie. Nina. Barbara.
Nathalie. Faith. Jan. Cheng Ch'ing Mao.
Terri. Mic. Isabel. Ron. Maurice. Cate.
Lisa. Nancy. Kelley. Alison. Joel.
Jenny. Richard. Jaki. Sally. Sylvia. Valerie. Melissa.
David. Glenn. Mimi. Jan. Sarah. Jack. Danny. Maureen.
Chas. Elaine. Marlene. Natasha. Pam.
Billy. Tokyo. Barry. Gregory. Dean. Phil.
Cathy. Sue. Chana. Kim. Carolyn. Marilyn.
Paula Dawn. Kathryn.
Paloma. Sara. Lawrence. Kerry. Marcy.
LaNelle. Mariah. Mary Ann. Sharon. Sarah.

Anora Sutherland

International travel, culture, languages are in the very air that Anora Sutherland breathed. She studied Italian, Arabic, French, Spanish, Latin and Mandarin Chinese, with a tiny foray into Tibetan.

The first of four children raised in a diplomatic family in the Middle East, her mother is half Italian, also the daughter of a diplomat, and she married a Middle Eastern specialist / lawyer, who joined the US Foreign Service.

Her father loved words, and his father before him. Songs. Rhymes. Humor. Her mother loves beauty and graciousness, and has a profound compassion that lives within the pragmatism that has taken care of her and her four little ones, all grown now, with three grandchildren.

Anora majored in Chinese, spent two years overseas in East Asia, including one in China, in Beijing in 1981, just a few years after the deadly Cultural Revolution had ended. Her son's father is Chinese from Taiwan. They divorced in the mid-1990s. Anora spent three years as a non-resident Buddhist nun in the United States. Anora remarried in 2007 to a global nomad who is half Japanese from North Carolina.

With a love of birds and gardens, trees and big blue cloudy skies, Anora divides her time between her online publicity work, and her literary journal, *When Women Waken*, her writing, wonderful friends and family. She has one grown son, a photographer, and lives with her husband and rescued beagle in central North Carolina.

Anora publishes her personal work under her maiden name, Anora Sutherland, and her business work under Anora McGaha.

The Blessing: A Fairy Tale about Grief
Author: Anora Sutherland

When Women Waken issues 2013-2016
Founding Editor / Publisher: Anora McGaha

Social Media for Business
Authors: Martin Brossman & Anora McGaha

Paula Dawn Lietz

The four photos for the cover were licensed from Canadian Artist Photographer Paula Dawn Lietz.

Paula Dawn Lietz is a published poet and an accomplished multi-genre artist and photographer specializing in digital media. Lietz has garnered extensive credits working with publishers and authors across nations. She revels in the creative energy generated within the artistic and literary community.

PD Lietz' artwork and photographs are widely sought after and are used for book covers, illustrations and other design projects. Lietz is known for her stylistic versatility and pristine work ethic. Her poet's heart shines through her visual interpretations of the world around her. Lietz creates unique work. She is considered an *outsider artist* in every sense of the word.

Lietz lives and works in Canada.

www.pdlietzphotography.com

Here's to you…

Reading changes lives.
Writing changes lives.
Publishing changes lives.

baddb

love you moon
love you rainman
love you j
love you mum
miss you mic
miss you kev

www.ingramcontent.com/pod-product-compliance
Lightning Source LLC
Chambersburg PA
CBHW020422230426
43663CB00007BA/1279